Karenrowe 5184 @ gm.

LETTERS
—FROM—
GALVESTON

LETTERS
—FROM—
GALVESTON
A Memoir

KAREN PAYSSE ROWE

Library of Congress Control Number: 2015904867
ISBN: Hardcover   978-1-5035-5724-6
                    Softcover   978-1-5035-5725-3
                    eBook   978-1-5035-5726-0

Rev. date: 04/08/2015

To order additional copies of this book, contact:
Xlibris
1-888-795-4274
www.Xlibris.com
Orders@Xlibris.com
705105

Dedication

John, Angie, Josh & Doll

January 4, 1942

Dear Wanda,

Thank you a heap for the nice Christmas card; I enjoyed it and your little note very much.

Don't worry about the misery you caused in lab, for I always looked forward to the lab afternoon as a day of fun. It's a wonder the whole bunch of us didn't get kicked out for raising so much cain. I saw Billy while I was home for the holiday, and he is just the same as ever. He is working for the City of Dallas now.

I still like to hunt and fish as much as ever, and I don't have any wife to fuss at me about going. Tell your papa that I still want to go hunting with him sometime if he will let me.

I guess you wonder what I am doing in Galveston. Well, I'm in med school, and it surely is swell. I started in June last summer, and I am nearly through with the first year now. I'll make a deal with you. If you will drum me up some patients in Fairfield or Wortham, I will buy some insurance from you. How's that?

SMU was all out for the Christmas holiday when I got home, so I didn't get to see anyone when I went out there.

It's time to go to bed now, and I have to go to school early tomorrow morning, so I had better quit. If you ever have any spare time, I would like very much to hear from you again.

Sincerely,
Ed Rowe

PS: When I went through Navasota on the train, I could at best see it, and that's more than I can say for Wortham.

Ed

January 4, 1942

Dear Wanda:

Thank you a heap for the nice Christmas card; I enjoyed it and your little note very much.

Don't worry about the misery you caused in lab, for I always looked forward to the lab afternoon as a day of fun. Its a wonder the whole bunch of us didn't get kicked out for raising so much cain. I saw Billy while I was home for the holidays, and he is just the same as ever. He is working for the City of

3

Dallas now.

I still like to hunt and fish as much as ever, and I don't have any wife to fuss at me about going. Tell your Papa that I still want to go hunting with him some time if he will let me.

I guess you wonder what I am doing in Galveston. Well, I'm in med school, and it surely is swell. I started in June last summer, and I am nearly through with the first year now. I'll make a deal with you. If you will drum me up some patients in Fairfield or Wortham, I will buy

3.

some insurance from you. Hows that?

S. M. U. was all "out" for the Christmas Holiday when I got home, so I didn't get to see anyone when I went out there.

Its time to go to bed now, and I have to go to school early tomorrow morning, so I had better quit. If you ever have any spare time, I would like very much to hear from you again.

Sincerely,

Ed. Rawe

P.S. When I went through Navasota on the train I could at least see it, and that's more than I can say for Wortham.

Ed.

Dear Wanda,

How much do you have in that diary anyhow? I hope you didn't mention all the times that I got so mean in lab, for I was mainly fooling all the time. Dr. Cheatum is the same as ever and just as absentminded. I don't know if you heard or not, but now he has a young son by the name of Dan, and he really is a little bugger. I went fishing with the Cheatums this summer and had a terrific job keeping Dan out of the lake. I think that I made a good nursemaid for him.

You're quite right. I never could forget about Ethel Claire. She was so funny in lab. I used to get a big kick out of the fight that she and Grubby got into. The last time I saw Grubby, he said something about her and wished he could see her again.

I am glad to hear that Billy is doing so well, but I knew that he would have no trouble going to college if he was half as good as you said he was. Even though I am so close to Houston, I hardly ever get up there; but the next time I go, I will get in touch with him. I would really like to know him. When I was coming home for Thanksgiving this year, there was quite a bunch of boys from Rice on the train with me. They were mostly members of the freshman football team, but I guess Billy was not among them, for they all went to Dallas. Be sure to tell Billy hello for me when you write him.

This has been a perfect weekend, for we do not have our regular quiz tomorrow and so we did not have to do any studying. I have been living like a huge king. Yesterday I played golf, and today I played tennis. It was so warm today that a bunch of boys from our house went swimming.

I guess you wonder where I am living. Well, I joined Phi Beta Pi Fraternity, and I am living in the fraternity house. The boys are all the swellest fellows, so we really have a good time.

Last night, we had a good dance and sort of a buffet supper at the house, and everybody had a keen time. I wish that you could have been here to go to the party; I know you would have enjoyed it. (Old maids do dance, don't they?)

Last Saturday, I got my grades and found that I had passed all my work for the preceding quarter, and that made me feel very good. I don't guess that Uncle Sam will get us until we graduate, but then he will be waiting for us in a big way. The way we are hurrying along now, I will be through down here in about two more years. Fairfield does sound pretty good as a place to practice, but I might have to go to Navasota. However, if more doctors come to Navasota, I guess that I will come to Fairfield if the people will promise not to run me out of town because I came from the lower regions of South Texas.

I had better quit for this time because I have to go up to the emergency room at the hospital for a while. If I can ever get up as far as Fairfield or Wortham, will you let me come to see you?

Please give your family my regards when you see them.

Yours,
Ed

PS: I will make peace if you will, and we won't talk about our hometowns anymore. Is that a deal?

Ed

January 18, 1942

Dear Wanda:

How much do you have in that diary anyhow? I hope you didn't mention all the times that I got so mean in lab, for I was mainly fooling all the time. Dr. Cheatum is the same as ever and just as absent-minded. I don't know if you heard or not, but now he has a young son by the name of Dan, and he really is a little booger. I went fishing with the Cheatums this summer and had a terrific job keeping Dan out of the lake. I think that I made a good nurse-maid for him.

you're quite right. I never could forget about Ethel Claire, she was so funny in fab. I used to get a big kick out of the fight that she and Hubby got into. The last time I saw Hubby, he said something about her, and wished he could see her again.

I am glad to hear that Billy is doing so well, but I knew that he would have no trouble going to college if he was half as good as you said he was. Even though I am so close to Houston, I hardly ever get up there, but the next time I go I will get in touch with him. I

would really like to know him. When [3]
I was coming home for Thanksgiving this
year there was quite a bunch of boys
from Rice on the train with me. They
were mostly members of the freshman
football team, but I guess Billy was
not among them, for they all went
to Dallas. Be sure to tell Billy hello
for me when you write him.

This has been a perfect week-end,
for we do not have our regular quiz
tomorrow, and so we did not have
to do any studying. I have been
living like a huge King. Yesterday
I played golf and today I played

tennis. It was so warm today that
a bunch of boys from our house went
swimming.

I guess you wonder where I am
living. Well, I joined Phi Beta Pi
fraternity, and I am living in the
fraternity house. The boys are all the
swellest fellows, so we really have a
good time.

Last night we had a good dance
and sort of a buffet supper at the
house, and everybody had a keen time.
I wish that you could have been
here to go to the party, I know you
would have enjoyed it. (old maids do
dance, don't they?)

Last Saturday I got my grades and found that I had passed all my work for the preceding quarter, and that made me feel very good. I don't guess that Uncle Sam will get us until we graduate, but then he will be waiting for us in a big way. The way we are hurrying along now, I will be through down here in about two more years. Fairfield does sound pretty good as a place to practice, but I might have to go to Navasota. However, if more doctors come to Navasota, I guess that I will come to Fairfield if the people will promise not to run me out of town because I came from the lower regions of South Texas.

I had better quit for this time, because I have to go up to the emergency room at the hospital for a while. If I can ever get up as far as Fairfield or Wortham, will you let me come to see you?

Please give your family my regards when you see them.

Yours,
Ed.

P.S. I will make peace if you will, and we won't talk about our home towns any more. Is that a deal?

Ed.

February 2, 1942

Dear Wanda,

Thank you a heap for the nice compliment about my letters. Now let me say the same thing about yours.

It sounds as though your home town was in quite an uproar; I know you had a swell time at meeting in Temple, and I know that all the Temple people got a good impression of the "girl from Freestone County."

Please excuse me for not telling you about my school sooner. Well, I guess that I'll confess that I am now a tea sipper since my school is the medical branch of the University of Texas. It is a pretty good school in spite of all that you might hear about it. There is a John Sealy Hospital here, and it is a part of the medical school. The school, hospital, and nurses' home are all built together in about four or five blocks, and they all work with each other.

There is a girl in our class from San Antonio, but she is not married, so I guess she is not the one whom you knew. She is quite the topic of conversation around our house, for she is a swell girl, and then my roommate is courting her fiercely nowadays. She is a very shy little girl, and my roommate is a very shy little boy, so the two of them take quite a bit of kidding from all sides.

The work is all swell here. I have just about finished the first year, and by next Christmas, I will be a junior; then after that, I will have only a year and a half to go. That is, I have about a little more than two years to go now, then I will have to serve two years of internship before I can practice. However, we will all probably serve in the army or navy, so there is not much telling when I will get to do some doctoring on my own.

This morning, I saw a swell operation. A Negro man had his leg amputated just a little above the knee. This was the first amputation that I have seen, and I was surprised at the quickness with which it was done. It didn't even take an hour. I don't know whether you would have liked it or not, for it was not very neat.

I had a wonderful weekend since there was no quiz to study for. I just played around and had a big time. On Saturday afternoon and Sunday afternoon, I played tennis until I was so tired that I could scarcely walk home. If I don't stop all this playing and loafing pretty soon, I am liable to flunk out of school. I have decided to study hard this week and catch up with everything. I will let you know if I stick to my resolution or not.

Tomorrow, we have to operate on dogs all day, so I had better quit and get some sleep, or else I will probably kill my poor dog.

I always enjoy hearing from people in the United States, so let me know about the news in Fairfield.

Yours,
Ed

February 2, 1942

1

Dear Wanda:

Thank you a heap for the nice compliment about my letters. Now, let me say the same thing about yours!

It sounds as though the one-horse town was in quite an uproar; I know you had a swell time at meeting in Temple, and I know that all the Temple people got a good impression of the "girl from Iveston County".

Please excuse me for not telling you about my school sooner. Well, I guess that I'll confess that I am now a tea-sipper, since my school is the medical branch of the University of Texas? It is a pretty good school in spite of all that you might hear about it. There is a John Sealy Hospital here, and it is a part of the medical school. The school, hospital, and nurses home are all built together in about four or five blocks, and they all work with each other.

There is a girl in our class from San Antonio, but she is not married, so I guess she is not the one whom you knew. She is quite the topic of conversation around our house, for she is a swell girl, and then my room mate is courting her

fiercely now-a-days. She is a very
shy little girl and my room-mate is
a very shy little boy, so the two
of them take quite a bit of kidding from
all sides.

The work is all swell here. I have
just about finished the first year, and
by next Christmas I will be a junior,
then after that I will have only a
year and a half to go. That is, I have
about two ~~more~~ years to go now,
    a little more than
then I will have to serve two years
of internship before I can practice.
However, we will all probably serve
in the army or navy, so there is not
much telling when I will get to do

some doctoring on my own.   4

This morning I saw a swell operation. A negro man had his leg amputated just a little above the knee. This was the first amputation that I have seen, and I was surprised at the quickness with which it was done. It didn't even take an hour. I don't know whether you would have liked it or not, for it was not very neat.

I had a wonderful week-end since there was no quiz to study for. I just played around and had a big time. Saturday afternoon and Sunday afternoon I played tennis until I was so tired that I could scarcely walk home.

If I don't stop all this playing and loafing pretty soon, I am liable to flunk out of school. I have decided to study hard this week and catch up with everything. I will let you know if I stick to my resolution or not.

Tomorrow we have to operate on dogs all day, so I had better quit and get some sleep, or else I will probably kill my poor dog.

I always enjoy hearing from people in the United States, so let me know about the news in Fairfield.

Yours,
Ed.

February 28, 1942

Dear Wanda,

What a time we have been having for the past ten days! Our fraternity has had two big parties. We have had a bunch of quizzes, and then the big investigation by the legislative committee was held here; and that threw everyone into a big uproar, so I am just now getting around to catching up on my letter writing.

Even though it may not seem so, I really do have a heart after all. Down here, one must accustom oneself to seeing all sorts of operations and great amounts of sickness and suffering. If we did not so accustom ourselves to all this, then we would not be able to do our jobs as efficiently as we are required, so please don't think that I am heartless just because I watch a few operations.

I see that you are still building your brother up as big as ever. He must feel awfully proud to have you pulling for him in such a big way. Next year really ought to be a big one for him, and you can bet that I will be listening to the Rice games when he is playing. Tell him to give them the devil in all the games except the SMU game, then he can slack off a little.

I also had to register on the sixteenth of this month, but I hope I will get deferred until I graduate from school. I have been thinking seriously about joining the naval reserves, and I may do it yet. If I do join, I will get to remain in school and then will get to intern in the navy somewhere then will go on duty.

Last night, we had a big banquet here at the fraternity house for all our alumni. All the old Phi Betas who graduated long ago came back, and after supper, they told us many stories of their days as medical students. We all had a swell time. It is one of the finest professions I know about—this medical profession. Even though the older doctors have more to do than they can take care of, they still have time to take care of "their boys" in medical school, and they see to it that everything goes well with us.

In about two weeks, our final exam will start, and after they are over and if I pass them, I will be a sophomore. That sounds good to me. Besides, I might even get to go home for a few days between quarters—this sounds even better.

I have not heard any news from SMU for quite a while, but if I go have in March, I will find out all the gossip, then I will let you know about all our good Dallas friends.

One of the boys just came in to borrow some of my roommate's clothes. I guess you have heard about how boys at school always wear part of their own clothes and then whatever else they can borrow. If I ever move out of the house, I think it will take me about a week to round up all my clothes from all over the place. Most of the boys are asleep this afternoon, and the house is unusually quiet.

I walked into a room on the second floor a little while ago, and there I found one of the boys cutting another boy's hair. The radio was playing some swingy tune, and I don't know whether the "barber" knew it or not, but his hand in which he had the scissors was keeping time to the music and cutting hair all at once. You can imagine how wavy the other fellow's hair is now.

Suppertime is here, so I had better quit for this time.

Yours,
Ed

February 28, 1942

Dear Wanda:

1

What a time we have been having for the past ten days. Our fraternity has had two big parties, we have had a bunch of quizzes, and then the big investigation by the legislative committee was held here, and that threw everyone into a big uproar, so I am just now getting around to catching up on my letter writing.

Even though it may not seem so, I really do have a heart after all. Down here one must accustom himself to seeing all sorts of operations and great amounts of sickness and suffering. If we did not so accustom ourselves to all this; [2] then we would not be able to do our jobs as efficiently as we are required, so please don't think that I am heartless just because I watch a few operations.

I see that you are still building your brother up as big as ever. He must feel awfully proud to have you pulling for him in such a big way. Next year really ought to be a big one for him, and you can bet that I will be listening to the Rice games when he is playing. Tell him to give them the devil in all the games except the S. M. U. game; then he can slack off a little.

I also had to register on the 16th of this month; but I hope I will get deferred until I graduate from school. I have been thinking seriously about joining the Naval Reserves, and I may do it yet. If I do join, I will get to remain in school, and then will get to intern in the navy somewhere, then will go on duty.

Last night we had a big banquet here at the fraternity house for all our alumni. All the old Phi Betas who graduated long ago came back, and after supper they told us many stories of their days as medical students.

We all had a swell time. It is one of the finest professions I know about — this medical profession. Even though the older doctors have more to do than they can take care of, they still have time to take care of "their boys" in medical school, and they see to it that everything goes well with us.

In about two weeks, our final exams will start, and after they are over, and if I pass them, I will be a sophomore. That sounds good to me. Besides, I might even get to go home for a few days between quarters — this sounds even better.

I have not heard any news from S.M.U. for quite a while, but if I go home in March I will find out all[5] the gossip, then I will let you know about all our good Dallas friends.

One of the boys just came in to borrow some of my room-mates' clothes. I guess you have heard about how boys at school always wear part of their own clothes and then whatever else they can borrow. If I ever move out of the house, I think it will take me about a week to round up all my clothes from all over the place. Most of the boys are asleep this afternoon, and the house is unusually quiet.

I walked into a room on the second ⁶ floor a little while ago, and there I found one of the boys cutting another boys' hair. The radio was playing some swingy tune, and I don't know whether the "barber" knew it or not, but his hand in which he had the scissors was keeping time to the music and cutting hair all at once. You can imagine how wavy the other fellow's hair is now.

Supper time is here, so I had better quit for this time.

Yours,
Ed.

29

Dear Wanda,

Do you remember what a jittery time final exam week was in college? Well, I feel just that way now, for we are right in the middle of our finals. I have just finished studying histology, and man, am I tired of that stuff. Tomorrow, my roommate and I have to learn about a million slides for the microscopic exam. All the exams will be over for us on Friday. Then if I did not fail anything, I will be a sophomore.

Usually we get a little time off between quarters, but this time we have to start right back to work again, so I won't even get to budge out of this bug-infested island.

I enjoyed your letter very much, but I was sorry to hear about you and your Aggie; that is, I was sorry for you. However, I couldn't help feeling just a little glad for myself since I might have a little bit of a chance now. He must be a funny fellow to let you go for someone else. You will have to tell me all about it sometime.

I wish that you could be here for the celebration, which is going to take place when finals end. On Saturday night, there is going to be a big dance. Every year at this time, all the fraternities go in together on a dance; and from what the older boys tell me, it is really something. Do you ever get to take the weekends off? If you do, I surely would like for you to come to Galveston to some of our parties. When the fraternity fixes out its schedule of parties and dances for the spring and summer, I will find out when something special is going to happen then maybe you could come down. How about it?

The weather has finally become warm, and the past week has been beautiful. It makes me want to do anything but sit in the house and study. Pretty soon, it will be time to go to the beach and swim. Some of my good fraternity brothers have bought a sailboat, and I think I will have to steal aboard and go for a ride in the bay pretty soon.

Thank you very much for the invitation to come to Wortham. I surely would like to see you, but as yet, I don't know whether we will get any time off at Easter or not. As soon as I find out for sure, I will let you know what I can do. What would your mama and papa say if I come to see you? They don't even know me.

It's about 12:30 now, so I had better quit, or else I won't even be able to look through a microscope tomorrow.

Please don't feel obligated to wait as long as I did to answer; I won't do it again.

Yours,
Ed

March 17, 1942

Dear Wanda:

Do you remember what a jittery time final exam week was in College? Well, I feel just that way now, for we are right in the middle of our finals. I have just finished studying histology, and man, am I tired of that stuff. Tomorrow, my room mate and I have to learn about a million slides for the microscopic exam. All the exams will be over for us Friday, then if I did not fail anything, I will be a sophomore.

Usually we get a little time off

between quarters, but this time we[2] have to start right back to work again, so I won't even get to budge out of this bug-infested island.

I enjoyed your letter very much, but I was sorry to hear about you and your Aggie; that is, I was sorry for you, however, I couldn't help feeling just a little glad for myself, since I might have a little bit of a chance now. He must be a funny fellow to let you go for someone else. You will have to tell me all about it sometime.

I wish that you could be here for the celebration which is going to take place when finals end. Saturday night there is going to be a big dance. Every year at this time all the fraternities go in together on a dance, and from what the older boys tell me, it is really something. Do you ever get to take the week ends off? If you do, I surely would like for you to come to Galveston to some of our parties. When the fraternity fixe out its schedule of parties and dances for the spring and summer, 4 I will find out when something special is going to happen; then maybe you could come down, how about it?

The weather has finally become warm, and the past week has been beautiful. It makes me want to do anything but sit in the house and study. Pretty soon it will be time to go to the beach and swim. Some of my good fraternity brothers have bought a sail boat, and I think I will have to steal aboard and go for a ride in the bay pretty soon.

Thank you very much for the invitation to come to Wortham. I surely would like to see you, but as yet I don't know whether we will get any time off at Easter or not. As soon as I find out for sure, I will let you know what I can do. What would your Mama + Papa say if I came to see you, they don't even know me?

It's about 12:30 now, so I had better quit, or else I won't even be able to look through a microscope tomorrow.

Please don't feel obligated to wait as
long as I did to answer; I won't do it
again.

Yours,
Ed.

Dear Wanda,

Here it's almost time to be going home. That really sounds good to me, for I haven't been home since Christmas. I am going to leave Friday morning, and I have to start back Monday, so I don't guess I will get to stop by Fairfield or Wortham this time. While I am home, I have to see about joining the navy, and I don't know how long that will take. I certainly will come up to see you though the first time I get a chance.

You said that you got the eighteenth to the twenty-fifth of May for a vacation. I'm not sure, but I believe that is when our next batch of finals will be coming off. If I find that this is not the case, then maybe you could come down over that weekend. Don't worry about a place to stay; I am sure I can find one. I guess you remember Charlie Sprague. He and his wife live here in Galveston, and you could most likely stay with them. I hope that our finals won't come until sometime in June, but I will let you know for sure as soon as I find out.

Tonight it seems as though the holidays have suddenly started, for everyone has already started raising the devil. I thought that I would study, but I don't believe that I will after all.

You must have really had quite a weekend when you went home. It always makes me feel pretty good to get together with a bunch of old friends. With Billy there too, it must have been swell.

I had to stop writing a minute to throw some firecrackers at my roommate while he was in the shower. You should have seen him jump.

What about those songs you were going to give Tommy Dorsey? Did you write them? If you did, you will have to show them to me sometime, will you?

Our sophomore work is very interesting and very hard, so I will really be glad to get into it and get it over.

I think there is a party in the making downstairs, so I had better see what is going on, then I have to go to the hospital for a while. I will write and tell you all the Dallas news when I come back.

Yours,
Ed

April 1, 1942

1

Dear Wanda:

Here it almost time to be going home. That really sounds good to me, for I haven't been home since Christmas. I am going to leave Friday morning, and I have to start back Monday, so I don't guess I will get to stop by Fairfield or Wortham this time. While I am home I have to see about joining the navy, and I don't know how long that will take. I certainly will come up to see you though, the first time I get a chance.

You said that you got the 18th to
the 25th of May for a vacation. I'm
not sure, but I believe that is when
our next batch of finals will be
coming off. If I find that this is
not the case, then maybe you
could come down over that week-
end. Don't worry about a place
to stay, I am sure I can find one.
I guess you remember Charlie Sprague.
He and his wife live here in
Galveston, and you could most
likely stay with them. I hope
that our finals won't come until
in June sometime, but I will let
you know for sure as soon as I

find out.

Tonight it seems as though the holidays have suddenly started, for everyone has already started raising the devil. I thought that I would study, but I don't believe that I will after all.

You must have really had quite a week-end when you went home. It always makes me feel pretty good to get together with a bunch of old friends. With Billy there too, it must have been swell.

I had to stop writing a minute to throw some fire crackers at my roommate while he was in the shower.

you should have seen him jump. &
What about those song you were
going to give Tommy Dorsey? Did you
write them? If you did you will
have to show them to me sometime;
will you?

Our sophomore work is very
interesting and very hard, so I will
really be glad to get into it and
get it over.

I think there is a party in the
making down stairs so I had better
see what is going on, then I have to
go to the hospital for a while. I will
write and tell you all the Dallas
news when I come back.   Yours,
                                    Ed.

April 20, 1942

Dear Wanda,

Everything was just swell in Dallas on Easter; I really had a good time going around to see all my old friends. I went out to school one day and saw Dr. Cheatum and Dr. Longnecker, and as usual, they about talked my head off. I went down to Dr. Cheatum's house and saw his new son, who is surely a cute little fellow. There were not any students at school the day I went, although I doubt if I would have known any of the new students anyhow. Dr. Cheatum and Dr. Longnecker said for me to give you their regards.

Besides seeing a bunch of people, I spent a good bit of time sleeping, for I was somewhat behind and needed to catch up.

I intended to ride the Southern Pacific home, and I would have looked around at Wortham (if I could have found it) while the train stopped there; but the bus driver in Houston gave my suitcase to a woman, and by the time I finally caught up with her and got it back again, the train had already left. I passed through on the way back to Galveston, but I didn't get to see much as the train was going too fast.

I would have had a much better time if I had gotten to see you, for it has certainly been entirely too long since I have seen you.

We are in about the same situation that you are in up there; only there are not any girls down here, and there are plenty of men. You should be down here; it would help even things up. One of our boys who is a weight lifter just came into the room. You ought to see him; he has more muscles than Charles Atlas.

I haven't heard about girls being drafted into the army, but it doesn't seem too improbable. Anyhow, if they do, we will certainly have a fine army. I guess that in spite of all I can do, they are going to make a doctor out of me before they let me in the army. I guess that will be all right, for we will be needed much more then than we are now.

When I got back to Galveston, I ran right into a hornet's nest. We have been having so much to do that we hardly have time to sleep. Today we had three quizzes, and when I got home, I took a long nap all afternoon long.

The weather has been beautiful and warm lately. On Saturday, just when we were getting all set to go swimming at the beach, we received a call that we had to come to the hospital for an autopsy, so that's where we spent our afternoon.

We got our last grades the other day, and I passed everything, so I was quite happy about that.

Tonight, we are having a stag party for the Phi Chi Fraternity, and I have to go down to help get things started right away, so good-bye until next time.

Yours,
Ed

April 20, 1942

1

Dear Wanda:

Everything was just swell in Dallas Easter; I really had a good time going around to see all my old friends. I went out to school one day and saw Dr. Cheatum and Dr. Longnecker, and as usual they about talked my head off. I went down to Dr. Cheatum's house and saw his new son; he is surely a cute little fellow. There were not any students at school the day I went, although I doubt if I would have known

any of the new students anyhow.
Dr. Cheatum and Dr. Longnecker
said for me to give you their
regards.

Besides seeing a bunch of people, I
spent a good bit of time sleeping,
for I was somewhat behind and
needed to catch up.

I intended to ride the Southern
Pacific home, and I would have
looked around at Marlham (if I
could have found it) while the train
stopped there, but the bus driver
in Houston gave my suitcase to
a woman, and by the time I
finally caught up with her and

get it back again, the train had already left. I passed through on the way back to Galveston, but I didn't get to see much, as the train was going too fast.

I would have had a much better time if I had gotten to see you, for it has certainly been entirely too long since I have seen you.

We are in about the same situation that you are in up there, only there are not any girls down here, there are plenty of men. You should be down here; it would help

even things up. One of our boys
who is a weight lifter just
come into the room. You ought
to see him; he has more
muscles than Charles Atlas.

I haven't heard about girls being
drafted into the army, but it
doesn't seem too improbable. Anyhow
if they do, we will certainly
have a fine army. I guess that
in spite of all I could, they
are going to make a doctor
out of me before they let me
in the army. I guess that
will be all right, for me

will be needed much more then
than we are now.

When I got back to Galveston, I
ran right into a hornet's nest. We
have been having so much to do,
that we hardly have time to
sleep. Today we had three
quizzes, and when I got home
I took a long nap all afternoon
long.

The weather has been beautiful
and warm lately. Saturday just
when we were getting all set
to go swimming at the beach, we
received a call that we had to

come to the hospital for an autopsy, so that's where we spent our afternoon.

We got our last grades the other day, and I passed everything, so I was quite happy about that.

Tonight we are having a stag party for the Phi Chi fraternity, and I have to go down to help get things started right away, so goodbye until next time.

Yours,
Ed.

May 12, 1942

Dear Wanda,

I hope you didn't think that I got lost or something means I haven't written in so long really. We have had so much work to do lately that I have scarcely had time to do anything. It seems that every time we get some time off, we have to do an autopsy. They certainly do place those things at the wrong time. But this is enough of excuse making. I think that from now until finals, we will have a little more time. Hope so anyhow.

The weather has been beautiful for quite a while now, and swimming season is going full blast. I have taken off two afternoons and gone to the beach, and it was surely swell. It makes one feel 100 percent better to get out in the fresh air after one has been in the house all winter.

What's this about your volunteering for the service? I haven't heard anything like that before. I am going to get in some branch of the service right away soon. I believe that I will join the navy as it seems to be the best bet.

Tonight is a rather easy night on us, so I think I will do a little letter writing and also a little studying.

When you see your papa, tell him to catch a fish for me, for I don't guess I will be able to go until June. We get about two weeks off at the first of June. Doesn't that sound swell? I guess that we will have to come back to school a little early, though for at about the end of the two weeks, our fraternity is going to start rushing activities, and we all have to be here then. Also my roommate and I are going to have to move out of the fraternity house to make room for the new boys, so I guess we will have to hunt us a new place to stay real soon now.

I am so sleepy that I can hardly hold my eyes open now; I wonder how I will ever manage to read any bacteriology tonight.

It needs reading right bad though, so I guess that I had better wake up somehow.

This quarter, we haven't had much time to watch operations or go near the hospital too much, and I certainly do miss it a lot. I will really be glad to get this sophomore year over and done with.

I am glad that you will be able to go to Dallas on your vacation; I know you will have a swell time. Please tell all the Dallas folks hello for me, that is, the ones that you see and that I might know.

Last week, I was so busy that I didn't even write my mama her weekly letter, so I had better quit now so I can write her a few lines. Write and tell me about your trip to Dallas.

Yours,
Ed

May 12, 1942

Dear Wanda:

I hope you didn't think that I got lost or something because I haven't written in so long. Really, we have had so much work to do lately that I have scarcely had time to do anything. It seems that every time we get some time off, we have to do an autopsy. They certainly do place those things at the wrong time. But this is enough of excuse making. I think that from now until finals we will have a little more time. Hope so anyhow.

The weather has been beautiful for quite a while now, and swimming season is going full blast. I have taken off two afternoons and gone to the beach, and it was surely swell. It makes one feel 100% better to get out in the fresh air after he has been in the house all winter.

What's this about your volunteering for the service? I haven't heard anything like that before. I am going to get in some branch of the service right away soon. I believe that I will join the navy, as it seems to be the best bet.

Tonight is a rather easy night on us, so I think I will do a little letter writing and also a little studying.

When you see your Papa, tell him to catch a fish for me, for I don't guess I will be able to go until June. We get about two weeks off at the

2

ED.B.ROWE.

first of June. Doesn't that sound swell? I guess that we will have to come back to school a little early, though. for about the end of the two weeks our fraternity is going to start rushing activities, and we all have to be here then. Also my room-mate and I are going to have to move out of the fraternity House to make room for the new boys, so I guess we will have to hunt us a new place to stay real soon now.

I am so sleepy that I can hardly hold my eyes open now; I wonder how I will ever manage to read any bacteriology tonight. It needs reading right bad though, so I guess that I had better wake up somehow

This quarter we haven't had much time to watch operations or go near the hospital too much, and I certainly do miss it a lot. I will really be glad to get this sophomore year over and done with.

I am glad that you will be able to go to Dallas on your vacation; I know you will have a swell time. Please tell all the Dallas folks hello for me; that is the ones that you see and that I might know.

Last week I was so busy that I didn't even write my Mama her weekly letter, so I had better quit now so I can write her a few lines. Write and tell me about your trip to Dallas.

Yours,
Ed.

July 6, 1942

Dear Wanda,

I guess you think that I got lost or something like that, don't you? Well, I guess I did get a little lost in a few final exams, but now they are all over, and I am relatively free again. It surely is a wonderful feeling. Once more, I passed everything, so now I am in the second third of my sophomore year.

We got a little vacation right after finals, so I went home for about a week. While I was there, I got to go on a fishing trip for about two days, and I really did catch some fish. I hope that they have started biting for your papa by this time.

Since I have been back in Galveston, we have taken a new freshman class, and we have all been very busy with them—getting them started off right, giving them parties, and scaring them with talk about the terrible quizzes in med school. Now that is all over, and all of us have settled down to a more routine schedule.

We had Saturday off for the Fourth, but it rained all day and all day yesterday and is still raining today. The streets are all flooded—if it doesn't quit pretty soon, I am going to school in my bathing suit, for I get sopping wet every time I go out anyhow.

My group is up now for autopsy—that is, we have to do the next one, so I am expecting the phone to ring almost any minute; however, I have hopes that we won't have to go until sometime tomorrow. I hope the thing comes during school hours so that we will get to miss class.

Last time I wrote, I think I said something about getting in the navy. Well, I have changed, and now I am getting in the army. I will get to finish my school, but as soon as I graduate, I will be placed on active duty in the army, which is a good thing, for the army is a fine place to start practice.

59

You certainly do get around, don't you? I'll bet you old Horace Heidt was tickled to dance with you; I would have been if I had been in his place. I'll bet you told him all about the fine little town of Wortham, or were you afraid to mention such a place?

The waves in the Gulf have been breaking fine for the past few days, but it has been too rainy to go swimming, so we just stand on the top floor of the clinic building and watch them roll in and wish it would clear up. I was all set to go today, but a little while ago, it became a regular storm.

I guess you remember Billy Stallcup and Pat, don't you? They are engaged now, and I heard from them the other day. They are coming to Galveston next Thursday and will stay until Sunday; I guess it must be vacation time for them. It will really be good to see them, for it's been a year since I have seen them.

Take good care of the cotton insurance business and drop me a line when you have time.

Yours,
Ed

ED.B.ROWE.

July 6, 1942

Dear Wanda:

I guess you think that I got lost or
something like that, don't you? Well, I guess
I did get a little lost in a few final exams,
but now they are all over, and I am relatively
free again; it surely is a wonderful feeling.
Once more I passed everything, so now I am
in the second third of my sophomore
year.

We got a little vacation right after
finals, so I went home for about a week.
While I was there I got to go on a fishing
trip for about two days, and I really
did catch some fish. I hope that they
have started biting for your Papa by
this time.

Since I have been back in Galveston, we have taken a new freshman class, and we have all been very busy with them, getting them started off right, giving them parties, and scaring them with talk about the terrible quizzes in med school. Now, that is all over, and all of us have settled down to a more routine schedule.

We had Saturday off for the Fourth, but it rained all day, and all day yesterday, and is still raining today. The streets are all flooded — if it doesn't quit pretty soon, I am going to school in my bathing suit, for I get sopping wet every time I go out anyhow.

My group is up now for autopsy — that is, we have to do the next one, so I am expecting the phone to ring almost any minute; however, I have hopes that we

3

ED.B.ROWE.

won't have to go until sometime tomorrow. I hope the thing comes during school hours, so that we will get to miss class.

Last time I wrote, I think I said something about getting in the navy. Well, I have changed, and now I am getting in the army. I will get to finish my school, but as soon as I graduate, I will be placed on active duty in the Army, which is a good thing, for the Army is a fine place to start practice.

You certainly do get around, don't you? I'll bet you old Horace Heidt was tickled to dance with you; I would have been, if I had been in his place. I'll bet you told him all about the fine little town of Wortham, or were you afraid to mention such a place?

The waves in the Gulf have been breaking fine for the past few days, but it has been too rainy to go swimming, so we just stand on the top floor of the clinic building and watch them roll in, and wish it would clear up. I was all set to go today, but a little while ago, it came a regular storm.

I guess you remember Billy Stallcup and Pat, don't you? They are engaged now, and I heard from them the other day. They are coming to Galveston next Thursday and will stay until Sunday, I guess it must be vacation time for them. It will really be good to see them, for it's been a year since I have seen them.

Take good care of the cotton insurance business, and drop me a line when you have time. Yours, Ed.

July 22, 1942

Dear Wanda,

I certainly did enjoy your letter. I really didn't deserve to get it so quick, but I am very glad you wrote so quickly. I promise not to wait so long again, even though I am very late with this one already.

It didn't take long for things to go to humming again around school. Just now I was trying to figure out when I would find time to read three hundred pages of clinical pathology for a quiz next Monday. All of us got behind this week because we had to initiate the freshmen three nights, and naturally, we got no studying done. Tonight is the last of all that, and I think everyone (especially the freshmen) is glad.

I have joined the army and have already received my commission as a second lieutenant, but I will get to finish my degree before going on active duty. I will be in the medical corps, and there is no telling what I will have to do. Most likely, they will put me to work sweeping out the kitchen.

You had better take the advice of your mother and father and go on to school next year. It isn't everyone who gets a chance at an education, and all those who get the chance had better take advantage of it. You will have a fine time at Rice, and then you will have plenty of time to be "on your own" when you finish school. Be sure to let me know what you decide to do.

Pat and Bill came down for three days, and we had a good time. Bill is going to some naval training school right away, then I guess he will be in the navy for the rest of the war. I wish that he could have stayed around in Texas somewhere, for I know that he and Pat would like to get married. I gave them your regards, and they said to be sure and tell you hello for them. When they left, they were surely sunburned—they both looked a sight.

I just got back from supper, and boy, are the freshmen scared. All the upper classmen are making out like they are getting drunk, and the freshmen think that they will catch the devil, at least that's what I thought last year. The invitation won't begin until about 9:00 tonight, so I am going to try to read a little clinical pathology before I go over.

Take good care of the mighty little town of Fairfield and write when you get a chance. I will write again real soon.

Yours,

Ed

July 22, 1942

1

Dear Wanda:

I certainly did enjoy your letter; I really didn't deserve to get it so quick, but I am very glad you wrote so quickly. I promise not to wait so long again, even though I am very late with this one already.

It didn't take long for things to go to humming again around school. Just now I was trying to figure out when I would find time to read 300 pages of clinical pathology for a quiz next Monday. All of us got behind this week, because we had to initiate the freshmen three nights, and naturally we got no studying done

67

Tonight is the last of all that, and I ²
think everyone (especially the freshman) is
glad.

I have joined the army, and have
already received my commission as a
2nd lieutenant, but I will get to
finish my degree before going on active
duty. I will be in the medical corps,
and there is no telling what I will
have to do. Most likely they will put
me to work sweeping out the kitchen.

You had better take the advice
of your mother and father and go on to
school next year. It isn't everyone
who gets a chance at an education,
and all those who get the chance had
better take advantage of it. You will

have a fine time at Rice, and then
you will have plenty of time to be
"on your own" when you finish school.
Be sure to let me know what you
decide to do.

Pat and Bill came down for three
days, and we had a good time. Bill is
going to some naval training school
right away, then I guess he will be
in the navy for the rest of the war. I
wish that he could have stayed around
in Texas somewhere, for I know that
he and Pat would like to get married.
I gave them your regards, and they
said to be sure and tell you hello
for them. When they left, they were
surely sunburned – they both looked

69

a sight.

I just got back from supper, and boy are the freshmen scared. All the upper classmen are making out like they are getting drunk, and the freshmen think that they will catch the devil, at least thats what I thought last year. The initiation wont begin until about 9:00 tonight, so I am going to try to read a little clinical pathology before I go over.

Take good care of the mighty little town of Fairfield, and write when you get a chance. I will write again real soon.

Yours,
Ed

Dear Wanda,

I guess you were talking about the governor's election, weren't you? I hardly knew the election was going on. I have not read anything except the funny paper in so long that I don't know what's happening anywhere.

This week has been some fine time. On Wednesday night, we were called on an autopsy, and when it was over, we had another one. And when that was over, we had another one. It was two o'clock in the morning when I finally got through, and I haven't caught up on my sleep till yet. Then last night, we had another one. Some life, isn't it?

Tonight there is an all-school dance, and I have to go for a while; but I intend to be home as early as I can, for we have a terrific quiz in bacteriology this next Monday.

I'll bet Billy was glad to get home for a while, and I know everyone was glad to see him. I thought you told me he was sort of little, but I guess you didn't if he weighs 175 pounds. He should do all the good this year at Rice—guess I'll have to time in every now and then and see how he is doing.

Thank you very much for asking me to go to the game with you; I will be very glad to, so I guess you are stuck now. Just so it doesn't come during final exams, everything will be fine. In the meantime, I will try to make up my mind which team to root for.

Hey, what's all this about the publicity in Freestone County? If you get your picture put in the paper, you had better send me one—I want to see if those photographers up there can take good pictures.

I hope you liked *Reap the Wild Wind*. When it was in Galveston, I thought it was swell. Last night, I saw *Sergeant York*, and it was very good.

You should have been here to go swimming today—I didn't go, but my roommate told me the water was real blue and clear, and the waves were terrific.

I think we will get the whole month of September off. Won't that be swell? I can hardly wait to get back into the United States where it is cool and where there are no mosquitoes.

That was certainly a five bunch of signs and stars at the end of your letter; I have seldom heard anything to equal that.

PS: Hope you don't break the camera.

Yours,
Ed

August 1, 1942

1

Dear Wanda:

I guess you were talking about the governor's election, weren't you? I hardly knew the election was going on. I have not read anything except the funny paper in so long that I don't know what's happening anywhere.

This week has been some fine time. Wednesday night we were called on an autopsy, and when it was over we had another one, and when that was over we had another one. It was two o'clock in the morning when I finally got through, and I haven't caught up on my sleep till yet. Then last night we had another one - some life isn't it.

Tonight there is an all-school dance, and I have to go for a while, but I intend to be home as early as I can, for we have a terrific quiz in bacteriology this next Monday.

I'll bet Billy was glad to get home for a while, and I know everyone was glad to see him. I thought you told me he was sorta little, but I guess you didn't if he weighs 175 lbs. He should do all the good this year at Rice - guess I'll have to tune in every now and then and see how he is doing.

Thank you very much for asking me

to go to the game with you; I will be very glad to; so I guess you are stuck now. Just so it doesn't come during final exams, everything will be fine. In the meantime I will try to make up my mind which team to root for.

Hey, what's all this about the publicity in Sweetson County. If you get your picture put in the papers you had better send me one — I want to see if those photographers up there can take good pictures.

I hope you liked "Reap the Wild Wind". When it was in Galveston I thought it was swell.

Last night I saw "Sergeant York", and it was very good.

You should have been here to go swimming today - I didn't go, but my room-mate told me the water was real blue and clear, and the waves were terrific.

I think we will get the whole month of September off; won't that be swell. I can hardly wait to get back into the United States where it is cool, and where there are no mosquitoes.

That was certainly a fine bunch of signs and stars at the end of your letter; I have seldom heard anything to equal that.

P.S. - Hope you don't break the camera.

Yours,
Ed.

September 8, 1942

Dear Wanda,

I'll bet that I am in the dog house again, for it's been some time since your letter came. I really didn't forget to write; I have just been fighting with final exams and all the excess work that comes up at the end of the quarter. Now that is all over, and I am free and happy again. I will never know if I passed until I go back to school in October, but if I did happen to pass, I will get to start making the rounds in the hospital every day. All sweating and lab work is over now. Doesn't that sound swell?

I got home on Sunday night at about 9:30, and I have been sleeping since then. It has rained all the time I have been home, so I have not been able to go bird hunting yet.

What about all this moving to Houston business? Are you really going to move? Houston is a good place to live, but I believe you would like Wortham better, and I'll bet that your papa will hate to give up his bird dog and his hunting and fishing trips. I surely would if I were in his place. Let me know what is going to happen.

I hope that everything is going along swell with the cotton crop insurance—maybe that business will put Fairfield on the map sure enough.

Tell Billy hello for me—I guess he is already home, isn't he? I think someone told me that Rice would start sometime during the last of September.

I will get to be home until the first few days in October. Our school doesn't start anymore until October 5. We got the ruckus all straightened out down there and got some new men to run the school, so everything turned out to be OK now.

I just looked out the window, and the clouds are beginning to break up, so I might go hunting this afternoon—I got to go real soon or else bust a value.

Drop me a line or two if you can find a free moment. I will be home all September.

Yours,
Ed

September 8, 1942

Dear Wanda:

I'll bet that I am in the
dog house again, for its been some
time since your letter came. I
really didn't forget to write, I
have just been fighting with
final exams and all the extra
work that comes up at the
end of the quarter. Now that
is all over and I am free and
happy again. I will never
know if I passed until I
go back to school in October, but
if I did happen to pass, I will
get to start making the rounds
in the hospital every day. All

sweating and lab work is over now. Doesn't that sound swell?

I got home Sunday night about 9:30, and I have been sleeping since then. It has rained all the time I have been home, so I have not been able to go bird hunting yet.

What about all this moving to Houston business? Are you really going to move? Houston is a good place to live, but I believe you would like Wortham better, and I'll bet that your Papa will hate to give up his bird dog and his hunting and fishing trips. I

81

surely would if I were in his place. Let me know what is going to happen.

I hope that everything is going along swell with the cotton crop insurance — maybe that business will put Fairfield on the map sure enough.

Tell Billy hello for me — I guess he is already home, isn't he? I think someone told me that Rin would start sometime during the last of September.

I will get to be home until the first few days in October. Our school doesn't start any more until October the fifth.

We got the ruckus all straightened[4]
out down there, and got some
new men to run the school, so
everything aut to be O.K. now.

I just looked out the window,
and the clouds are beginning to
break up, so I might go
hunting this afternoon — I got to
go real soon or else bust a
valve.

Drop me a line or two if
you can find a free moment.
I will be home all September.
Yours,
Ed.

September 22, 1942

Dear Wanda,

For the past week, a friend of mine has been visiting me, and we have been running all over town going everywhere, so that's the reason for the delay in answering.

After I talked to you the other day, Mama said that you should have stayed overnight with us, so if you plan to come up anymore, well, why don't you do that next time? Mama practically beat me up for not saying something about it to you.

Since I have been home, I have been keeping busy, but it seems that I have done nothing as yet. I have not even been to see Dr. Cheatum; however, I have talked to him a couple of times. When I go out to school sometime this week, I will tell him hello for you. He will be glad to hear from you again.

I have been going out to Parkland Hospital quite a bit since I have been have, and the other night, I got to do some work in the emergency room. A Negro man had his lip and his head cut, and I sewed him up. That was the first bit of sewing I have done, but I got by all right; and the doctor told me to come back and work again whenever I could, so I am going back quite a few times before I go back to school.

I know that you and Doris Evelyn have a nice time living together in your own house. I would like to sneak in some day and eat dinner with you. I'll bet you two are good cooks.

If my aunt and uncle bring me back to school, I will stop by and say hello to you. I will let you know later whether they are going to bring me or not.

By some handful of bad luck, I was elected editor of our fraternity chapter, so now I have to get busy and write to the national editor and tell him all that has been going on during the summer—some stuff. The way I feel this time, it will be a very straight letter.

If I quit now, I will be able to get this letter off in the afternoon mail, so I will be looking forward to hearing from you again when you can find a spare moment to write.

Yours,
Ed

September 22, 1942

Dear Wanda,

For the past week a friend of mine has been visiting me, and we have been running all over town going everywhere, so that's the reason for the delay in answering.

After I talked to you the other day, Mama said that you should have stayed overnight with us, so if you plan to come up any more, well, why don't you do that next time. Mama practically beat me up for not saying something about it to you.

Since I have been home, I have been keeping busy, but it seems that I have done nothing as yet. I have not even been to see Dr. Cheatum; however, I have talked to him a couple of times. When I go out to school sometime this week, I will tell him hello for you. He will be glad to hear from you again.

I have been going out to Parkland Hospital quite a bit since I have been here, and the other night I got to do some work in the emergency room. A negro man had his lip and his head cut, and I sewed him up. That was the first bit of sewing I have done, but I got by all right, and the doctor told me to come back and work again whenever I could, so I am going back quite a few times before I go back to school.

I knew that you and Doris Evelyn have a nice time living together in your own house. I would like to sneak in some day and eat dinner with you. I'll bet you two are good cooks.

If my aunt and uncle bring me back to school, I will stop by and say hello to you. I will let you know later whether they are going to bring me or not.

By some handfull of lead luck I was elected editor of our fraternity chapter, so now I have to get busy and write to the national editor and tell him all that has been going on during the summer — some stuff. The way I feel this time it will be a very short letter.

If I quit now, I will be able to get this letter off in the afternoon mail, so I will be looking forward to hearing from you again when you can find a spare moment to write.

Yours,
Ed.

October 5, 1942

Dear Wanda,

Here I am back at school again. It seems that vacation doesn't last very long. Today was our first day, and they put us to work as usual. This afternoon I have been shopping around, looking at little white coats so they won't throw me out of the hospital tomorrow on my first ward rounds.

I surely was sorry to hear about your mother; hope she is much better now. Please give her my regards and tell her to get well in a hurry. Be sure to let me know how she is getting along. If I could have been of any help, I wish I could have been there too.

We had to be in Galveston today, so I left Dallas on Friday night and stayed all night with my aunt in Navasota. We came through Wortham late Friday night, but I didn't stop, for I know you were in Fairfield, and I didn't believe anyone would be home in Wortham anyhow. We seem to have a terrible time trying to see each other, but we will manage it soon, I just have a feeling.

The weather is very hot in Galveston, so yesterday afternoon, I went swimming and spent quite a time at the beach. The sun was so hot that I really got quite a sunburn. Guess that is the last sunburn I will get this year.

The grades for our summer work came out today, and I found that again I had passed all the work. If I keep on going to church every once in a while, I may even get out of this school before long. It seems that the administration is lightening up on its requirements now, for there were seven who busted out of our class this time. As you can imagine, that caused quite an uneasy feeling among those of us who are left. If I bust out anytime, guess I will have to be a farmer.

Take good care of yourself, don't work too hard, and write whenever you can find time.

Yours,
Ed

October 5, 1942

Dear Wanda:

Here I am back at school again. It seems that vacations don't last very long. Today was our first day, and they put us to work as usual. This afternoon I have been shopping around looking at little white coats, so they won't throw me out of the hospital tomorrow on my first ward rounds.

I surely was sorry to hear about your mother; hope she is much better now. Please give her my regards, and tell her to get well in a hurry. Be sure to let me know how she is getting along. If I could have been of any help, I wish I could have been there too.

We had to be in Galveston today, so I left Dallas Sunday night and stayed all night

with my aunt in Navasota. We came through
Wortham late Friday night, but I didn't stop
for I knew you were in Fairfield, and I didn't
believe anyone would be home in Wortham
anyhow. We seem to have a terrible time trying
to see each other, but we will manage it
soon, I just have a feeling.

The weather is very hot in Galveston, so
yesterday afternoon I went swimming and spent
quite a time at the beach. The sun was so
hot that I really got quite a sunburn. Guess
that is the last sunburn I will get this
year.

The grades for our summer work came out
today and I found that again I had passed
all the work. If I keep on going to church
every once in a while, I may even get out
of this school before long. It seems that
the administration is lightening up on its
requirements now, for there were seven who

GALVESTON, TEXAS

busted out of our class this time. As you can imagine, that caused quite an uneasy feeling among those of us who are left. If I bust out anytime, guess I will have to be a farmer.

Take good care of yourself, don't work too hard, and write whenever you can find time.

Yours,
Ed.

Dear Wanda,

What do you think? My auntie decided that I needed some respectable stationery, so she hauled off and gave me some.

This morning, we had to stay an hour later than usual in school, and we missed our dinner, so I was thinking things I shouldn't have when I came home and found your nice long letter, then I got in a real good humor. I'm glad the boss didn't catch you writing on government time and on Uncle Sam's paper. When I saw all the headlines on the envelope, I thought someone was after me for something, but I couldn't think of what.

I'm very glad to hear that your mother is so much better; that just goes to show you that it takes more than a little old operation to get a good "Worthamite" down. Boy! I'll bet she was glad to get home and away from the hospital with all its smells. I used to think that hospitals smelled bad, but now I have become rather numbed to any smells that might be present there. Please remember me to your mother when you go home next time. Also, tell your papa that I went fishing yesterday and caught a bunch of saltwater perch. That was my first fishing trip since I have been here, and I really did enjoy it. Guess I will go again soon now.

I listened to several football games Saturday afternoon, among them the Rice-Tulane game. It was a fairly good game, but I was very sorry to see Rice lose the game. Down here at school, we all pull for Rice and Texas above all the rest. When you write to Billy, tell him I'm very sorry but I won't be able to go to the Texas-Rice game, for it's too hard for us to get away from here on Saturday. We have quizzes on Monday and usually wind up doing a good bit of studying Saturday. I do wish I could go, and I wish you were able to go. We do have several weekends off this quarter, and maybe one of them falls on the weekend of the Rice-A&M game; if it does, I will holler loud. I will let you know just as soon as I find out, and I will know by the next time I write.

Please don't work too hard in the yard; I really need to get some good exercise, so I would be very glad to help you with the work if I were there.

You better be careful how you holler for Wortham at the Fairfield game, for some of those Fairfield people might kidnap you and get rid of you. Anyhow, I hope you have a good time and don't get run out of town. You should see our class since we have started working in the hospital wards. We all have to wear little white coats and carry a bunch of tools with us. I can't get accustomed to wearing a tie to school every day, but I guess I will before long. My first patient had TB, and you can rest assured that I handled him carefully to keep from getting the little bugs on me. My other patient fell over in the street unconscious one day, and we don't know just exactly what is the matter with him as yet.

This afternoon, I had to study my lessons for tomorrow so that I could spend my time tonight writing up a long history of my first patient. That is all very interesting, but it takes a very long time and a good bit of work. It is all fun, however.

It's nearly time for supper, so I had better quit for this time. Write again when you have time.

Yours,
Ed

October 12, 1942

E
B
R

Dear Wanda:

What do you think? My auntie decided that I needed some respectable stationery, so she hauled off and gave me some.

This morning we had to stay an hour later than usual in school, and we missed our dinner, so I was thinking things I shouldn't have when I came home and found your nice long letter, then I got in a real good humor. I'm glad the boss didn't catch you writing on government time and on Uncle Sam's paper. When I saw all the headlines on the envelope, I thought someone was after me for something, but I couldn't think of what.

I'm very glad to hear that your mother is so much better; that just goes to show you that it takes more than a little old operation to get a good "Warthenite" down. Boy! I'll bet she was glad to get home and away from the hospital with all its smells. I used to think that hospitals smelled bad, but now I have become rather numbed to any smells that might be present there. Please remember me to your mother

95

E
B
R

when you go home next time. Also tell your Papa that I went fishing yesterday and caught a bunch of salt water perch. That was my first fishing trip since I have been here, and I really did enjoy it. Guess I will go again soon now.

I listened to several football games Saturday afternoon, among them the Rice - Tulane game. It was a fairly good game, but I was very sorry to see Rice lose the game. Down here at school we all pull for Rice and Texas above all the rest. When you write to Billy, tell him I'm very sorry, but I won't be able to go to the Texas - Rice game, for its too hard for us to get away from here on Saturday. We have quizzes on Monday, and usually wind up by doing a good bit of studying Saturday. I do wish I could go, and I wish you were able to go. We do have several week-ends off this quarter, and maybe one of them falls on the week-end of the Rice - A & M game; if it does I will holler loud. I will let you know just as soon as I find out, and I will know by the next time I write.

Please don't work too hard in the yard; I really need to get some good exercise, so I would be very glad to help you with the work if I were there.

You better be careful how you holler for Wortham at the Fairfield game, for some of those Fairfield people might kidnap you and get rid of you. Anyhow, I hope you have a good time and don't get run out of town.

E
B
R

You should see our class since we have started working in the hospital wards. We all have to wear little white coats, and carry a bunch of tools with us. I can't get accustomed to wearing a tie to school every day, but I guess I will before long. My first patient had T.B., and you can rest assured that I handled him carefully to keep from getting the little "bugs" on me. My other patient fell over in the street unconscious one day, and we don't know just exactly what is the matter with him as yet.

This afternoon I had to study my lessons for tomorrow, so that I could spend my time tonight writing up a long history of my first patient. That is all very interesting, but it takes a very long time and a good bit of work. It is all fun, however.

It's nearly time for supper, so I had better quit for this time. Write again when you have time.

Yours,
Ed.

Dear Wanda,

I hate to think what you will say to me in your next letter, for I have waited too long to answer your last.

Since you last heard from me, I have been elected treasurer of the fraternity, and there has been one big hullabaloo trying to get the books all straightened out so I can take over the job. It's a pay job, so I will have to move back into the house again. Don't think I will move just yet, though.

I am very glad that you got to go to Houston to see the game. Bet you were sleepy when you finally got back home. It was a very good game, even though Rice did get whipped. I listened to part of it on the radio.

This weekend, half of our class went to Houston on a field trip, and we had a good time. We got to ride up and back in army trucks, and that made the trip all the more fun. We went through Ellington Field, the Hughes Tool Company, and the Grand Prize Brewery; then on the way home, we sang songs at the top of our voices. That was the first time I have been anywhere since I went home in September.

Tomorrow morning, I have to go on the hospital ward where all the crazy people are and learn how to do a physical and mental exam on them. That ought to be some fun. Hope they will let me out again.

All the seniors are throwing a big party at our house tonight, so I guess I will go. It is the custom for the seniors to give a party each year when they get their internships. I ran all the talk; this one tonight is really going to be a party. Too bad we have to go to school tomorrow.

We get off four days for Thanksgiving, but I guess I will stay in Galveston, for it is such a short time until Christmas. Anyhow, I have a little studying I need to catch up on before finals come around again, and they are coming too soon. It seems that all we do is take finals. Anyhow after Christmas, if I get promoted, I won't have to worry about any more quizzes on Monday; I will have the weekends free, and that sounds plenty good to me.

Please give all your family my regards and write when you can find a spare moment.

Yours,
Ed

November 16, 1942

Dear Wanda:

I hate to think what you will say to me in your next letter, for I have waited too long to answer your last.

Since you last heard from me, I have been elected treasurer of the fraternity, and there has been one big hullabaloo trying to get the books all straightened out so I can take over the job. Its a pay job, so I will have to move back into the house again. Don't think I will move just yet, though.

I am very glad that you got to go to Houston to see the game. Bet you were sleepy when you finally got back home. It was a very good game, even though Rice did get whipped. I listened to part of it on the radio.

This week end half of our class went to Houston on a field trip, and we had a good time. We got to ride up and back in army trucks, and that made the trip all the more fun. We went through Ellington Field, the Hughes Tool Company, and the Grand Prize Brewery; then on the way home we sang songs at the top of our voices. That was the first time I have been anywhere since I went home in September.

Tomorrow morning I have to go on the hospital ward where all the crazy people are, and learn how to do a physical and mental exam on them. That ought to be some fun. Hope they will let me out again.

All the seniors are throwing a big party at our house tonight, so I guess I will go. It is the custom for the seniors to give a party

each year when they get their internships.
I saw all the talk, this one tonight is really
going to be a party. Too bad we have to go
to school tomorrow.

We get off four days for Thanksgiving, but I
guess I will stay in Galveston, for it is such
a short time until Christmas. Anyhow I have
a little studying I need to catch up on before
finals come around again, and they are
coming too soon. It seems that all we do
is take finals. Anyhow after Christmas, if I
get promoted, I won't have to worry about
any more quizzes on Monday; I will have
the week ends free, and that sounds plenty
good to me.

Please give all your family my regards,
and write when you can find a spare
moment.

Yours,
Ed.

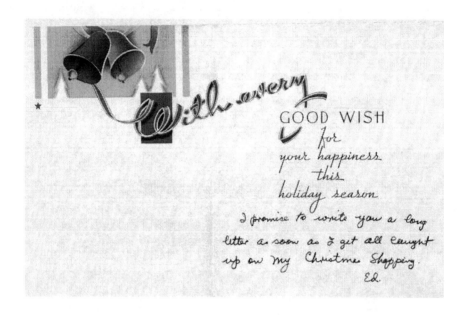

Good wish
for
your happiness
this
holiday season

I promise to write you a long letter as soon as I get all caught
up on my Christmas shopping.

Ed

January 17, 1943

Dear Wanda,

By this time, I don't know what you think of me, but I'll bet it's not very good. Thank you for your Christmas card and the nice note. I have finally gotten everything straightened out so that I at last will have a little free time. The fraternity finances have all been worked up-to-date, and I am at a loss getting used to the work in my new school year. This year, I have no quizzes to study for on the weekend, so I can rest and just have a good time in general. I even went so far as to go to church this morning.

The stay at home for two weeks was very fine, and I caught up on my sleep again. While I was home, I did a good bit of work in the hospital, and I had a good time doing it besides learning a great many helpful things. Then I even found time to go hunting a couple of times.

I went out to school one day and saw all the professors; they were all fine and are still teaching the same old stuff. I didn't see many of the kids as there are not many around the biology department anymore. I think Dr. Geiser scared everyone off. I did see Charles Wisseman while I was there. He has come back to Dallas now and has a job at Baylor Medical School. He will start medical school in June when the new class comes in.

Tell me about your Christmas holiday. I'll bet you had a good time with Billy at home and all. Did he really bring all the boys home with him like he said he would? I passed through Wortham on the train on the way home and on the way back. On the way back to school, I met a boy I knew who is going to Rice and who is on the football team. He said he knew Billy. His name is Nick Lanza. Did you meet him when you went to the game in Houston?

The medical work is just fine and is getting more interesting every day. I got my grades again the other day, and I passed all the subjects, so I am happy again.

If you are still on speaking terms with me after so long, please drop me a line sometime, and I promise to write real soon. Give my regards to your mother and dad.

Yours,
Ed

January 17, 1943

E
B
R

Dear Wanda:

By this time I don't know what you think of me, but I'll bet its not very good. Thank you for your Christmas card and the nice note. I have finally got everything straightened out so that I at last will have a little free time. The fraternity finances have all been worked up to date, and I am at last getting used to the work in my new school year. This year I have no quizzes to study for on the week end, so I can rest and just have a good time in general. I even went so far as to go to church this morning.

The stay at home for two weeks was very fine, and I caught up on my sleep again. While I was home, I did a good bit of work in the hospital, and I had a good time doing it besides learning a great many helpful things. Then I even found time to go hunting a couple of times.

I went out to school one day and saw all the professors; they were all fine and are still teaching the same old stuff. I didn't see many of the girls, as there are not many around the

107

Biology department any more. I think Dr. Geiser scared everyone off. I did see Charles Weiseman while I was there. He has come back to Dallas now, and has a job at Baylor Medical School. He will start to Medical school in June when the new class comes in.

Tell me about your Christmas holiday. I'll bet you had a good time with Billy at home and all. Did he really bring all the boys home with him like he said he was. I passed through Waxahom on the train on the way home and on the way back. On the way back to school I met a boy I knew who is going to Rice and who is on the football team. He said he knew Billy. His name is Nick Lanza - Did you meet him when you went to the game in Houston?.

The Medical work is just fine and is getting more interesting every day. I got my grades again the other day and I passed all the subjects, so I am happy again.

If you are still on speaking terms with me after so long, please drop me a line sometime, and I promise to write real soon. Give my regards to your mother and dad.

Yours,
Ed.

I can *tel-a-vision*
When I see one!

Won't you be
my
Valentine?

Ed Rowe

Dear Wanda,

Well, I have waited too long again, but here goes anyhow. I enjoyed your last letter very much, and I was glad to hear that everything is going all right with you except the cold weather. It got pretty cold here too—I really froze to death one night. I had to put on a whole bunch of clothes then wrap up in an overcoat to keep warm while I was studying. That's the only real cold spell we have had for quite a while—usually the weather is sort of warm.

For the past couple of weekends, it has been very pretty and warm, and I have gone to the beach. However, I did not go swimming—just watched the people haul in a big trout out of the Gulf. Guess I will have to go fishing some this spring.

The schoolwork has all been fine, although there has been quite a bit of it. I am working in the children's hospital now, and I enjoy it very much. I have one little two-year-old boy and one little Negro girl, four years old, as patients now. The little boy has fluid in his abdomen and is just about to get pneumonia now. I have to go see him in just a minute. The little Negro girl is just getting over a case of diphtheria. She probably wonders what I look like, for when I go to see her, I am all dressed up in a gown and have a mask pulled up over my face. It's a wonder I didn't scare her most to death. This next Thursday, I will go on obstetrics, and maybe I will get to deliver some young 'uns.

We have commenced to have too many pop quizzes to suit me lately; I wouldn't be surprised to get called in to the dean for flunking so many of them. One good thing is, we don't have to put up with grades anymore.

I hope you haven't had any more trouble with the water pipes—I'll bet you two are really something to watch, puttering around in that house.

It's almost time for class, and I have to go see one of my patients, so good-bye for this time. Drop me a line when you ever find time.

Yours,
Ed

February 15, 1948

Dear Wanda:

Well, I have waited too long again, but here goes anyhow. I enjoyed your last letter very much, and I was glad to hear that everything is going all right with you except the cold weather. It got pretty cold here too - I nearly froze to death one night. I had to put on a whole bunch of clothes then wrap up in an overcoat to keep warm while I was studying. That's the only real cold spell we have had for quite a while - usually the weather is sorta warm.

For the past couple week-ends it has been very pretty and warm, and I have gone to the beach. However, I did not go swimming - just watched the people haul in big boat out of the Gulf. Guess I will have to go fishing some this spring.

The school work has all been fine, although there has been quite a bit of it. I am working in the children's hospital now, and I enjoy it very much. I have one little 2-year old boy and one little negro girl 4 years old as patients now. The little boy has fluid in his abdomen, and is just about to get pneumonia now. I have to go see him in just a minute. The little Negro girl is just getting over a case of diptheria. She probably wonders what I look like, for when I go to see her, I am all dressed up in a gown and have a mask pulled up over my face. It's a wonder I didn't scare her most to death. This next Thursday I will go on obstetrics, and maybe I will get to deliver some youngsuns.

We have commenced to have too many pop-quizzes to suit me lately, I wouldn't be surprised to get called in to the dean for flunking so many of them. One good thing, we don't have to put up with grades any more.

I hope you haven't had any more trouble with the water pipes - I'll bet you two are really something to watch puttering around in that house.

It's almost time for class, and I have to go see one of my patients, so goodby for this time. Drop me a line when you can find time.

Yours,
Ed.

Dear Wanda,

I surely was glad to get your letter yesterday. No, I am not lost. I am still in the same old place, but I am in the army now. I am very sorry. I neglected to write to you in so long; I don't have any excuse. I just seemed to do something else, but I did think of you a lot in the meantime. Guess I will have to try to be real good about writing from now on.

On July 1, 1943, I got my orders to go to San Antonio for induction into the army. We spent about a week in San Antonio then came back to Galveston to school again. We have a good setup now. The government pays our tuition, our room and board, and fifty-four dollars per month. We have to go to school for roll call at 7:30 every morning, then we have an hour for military each afternoon and usually put in a couple of hours on Saturday afternoon.

We had been back in Galveston about two weeks when the storm hit. I was working on some patients in the hospital when it hit. The wind began to blow rain into the hospital, so I went to work morning patients out of the way. Then the windows began to blow out, and the water really came in. Up in the operating room, the lights went out while they were doing two operations, so they got flashlights; then the skylight fell in, and everyone had to get out of there. The roof blew off part of the hospital, and it sounded as if the whole place were falling down. We had to move all the patients out of the two top floors of the hospital and take them across the street to another building. The wind blew the bay right up into town and in front of the hospital; it was about five feet deep. In some places in town, the water was so deep people had to swim from place to place.

When the storm was finally over in the afternoon at about four o'clock, the people who had been hurt began to come in, and we patched them up by candlelight until the wee hours of the morning. The next morning I got home, and our house was a mess. All the rooms were drenched, for the storm blew off most of the roof. The window blew out of my room, and water blew all over everything. Nearly all my clothes got wet, and all my shoes were floating around the room in the water. We worked on the house for about a week and got it patched up, but it still leaks whenever it rains. The lights and water were off for over a week, so we got us a gasoline lamp and a kerosene lamp to find our way about with. I hope we don't have anything else like that anytime soon.

Well, I am a senior now, and the work is much more interesting than formerly. I have had a big bunch of patients lately, but today I finished working on them, so I am catching up on my letter writing now. I am working on the surgery wards, and I really have some messy patients. I had one with cancer of the ear; cancer of the face; osteomyelitis, hence, bunions, infantile paralysis, etc. Then every once in a while, I get to help on an operation.

How has everything been in Fairfield? Do you still work for the same company, and do you still keep house for yourself? When you have time, be sure to write and tell me all about yourself again.

Guess I had better quit for this time as it is late and I have a lot of fine sleeping to do, but I will write again soon.

Yours,
Ed

PS: In spite of all the addresses on the outside of the envelope, you can address your letters to Pfc. E. B. Rowe at 1228 Avenue D, Galveston, Texas.

Ed

August 10, 1943

Dear Wanda:

I surely was glad to get your letter yesterday. No. I am not lost, I am still in the same old place, but I am in the army now. I am very sorry I neglected to write to you in so long; I don't have any excuse, I just seemed to do something else, but I did think of you a lot in the meantime. Guess I will have to try to be real good about writing from now on.

About July 1, 1943, I got my orders to go to San Antonio for induction into the Army. We spent about a week in San Antonio, then came back to Galveston to school again. We have a good setup now. The government pays our tuition, our room and board, and $54 per month. We have to go to school for roll call at 7:30 every morning, then we have an hour for military each afternoon, and usually put in a couple of hours on Saturday afternoon.

We had been back in Galveston about two weeks when the storm hit. I was working on some

EDMUND JONES
Archon
DAVID DAWSON
Vice Archon

ALPHA KAPPA CHAPTER
PHI BETA PI

BRUCE CAMERON
Secretary
ED ROWE
Treasurer

2.

GALVESTON, TEXAS

patients in the hospital when it hit. The wind began to
blow rain into the hospital, so I went to work moving
patients out of the water. Then the windows began to blow
out, and the water really came in. Up in the operating
room, the lights went out while they were doing
two operations, so they got flash lights, then the
sky-light fell in, and everyone had to get out of
there. The roof blew off part of the hospital, and
it sounded as if the whole place were falling
down. We had to move all the patients out of
the two top floors of the hospital, and take them
across the street to another building. The wind blew
the bay right up into town, and in front of the
hospital, it was about 5 ft. deep. In some places
in town, the water was so deep people had to
swim from place to place.

When the storm was finally over in the afternoon
about 4:00 o'clock, the people who had been hurt
began to come in, and we patched them up by
candle-light until the wee-hours of the morning.
The next morning I got home, and our house was a
mess. All the rooms were drenched, for the storm

117

EDMUND JONES
Archon
DAVID DAWSON
Vice-Archon

ALPHA KAPPA CHAPTER
PHI BETA PI

BRUCE CAMERON
Secretary
ED ROWE
Treasurer

GALVESTON, TEXAS

3.

blew off most of the roof. The window blew out of my room, and water blew all over everything. Nearly all my clothes got wet and all my shoes were floating around the room in the water. We worked on the house for about a week, and got it patched up, but it still leaks whenever it rains. The lights and water were off for over a week, so we got us a gasoline lamp and a kerosine lamp to find our way about with. I hope we don't have anything else like that anytime soon.

Well, I am a senior now, and the work is much more interesting than formerly. I have had a big bunch of patients lately, but today I finished working on them, so I am catching up on my letter writing now. I am working on the surgery wards, and I really have some messy patients I had one with cancer of the ear, cancer of the face, osteomyelitis, hernia, burnians, infantile paralysis, etc. Then every once in a while I get to help on an operation.

How has everything been in Fairfield? Do you still work for the same company, and do you still keep house for yourself? When you have time, be sure to write and tell me all about yourself again.

Guess I had better quit for this time, as it is late and I have a lot of fine sleeping to do, but I will write again soon.

Yours,
Ed.

P.S. In spite of all the address on the outside of the envelope, you can address your letters to Pfc. E.B. Rowe 1228 Ave D., Galveston, Tx.

Ed.

September 1, 1943

Dear Wanda,

I believe you have the prettiest handwriting I have ever seen, and I surely do like to read it. That was a sweet long letter you wrote to me; I wish that I could think of that many interesting things to say. Last night I started a letter to you, but one of my good fraternity brothers came in, and the full session lasted into the night. I don't know how we can manage to waste so much time.

Last week the water finally cleared up in the Gulf, and I caught two nice strings of fish. We had a fishing trip all planned on Sunday morning, and we got up before daylight and started out; but we could not find any bait in all of Galveston, so we came back home and went to bed.

Here it is the opening day of dove season in Dallas County, and I am not there to help open it. I guess this is about the second time since I have been able to walk that I have missed opening day. Guess I will have to make up for lost time when I get out of school. The boy who started the bull session last night has invited me to go home with him this winter and do some duck hunting, and I am planning big on that.

A little while ago, I just came from the hospital where I have been helping to take blood from 360 draftees. Boy, I thought they would never quit coming through the door.

I have not heard from Pat and Bill for about six months now. Bill was in the Air Corps Ground School somewhere in Florida, I believe, and Pat is there with him.

For the past several days, I have been busy writing out applications for internship. I want to go to Parkland Hospital in Dallas, but I have applied at Denver and Iowa City in case I do not get in at Parkland. The army allows us a year for a civilian internship, during which time we may go to any hospital in the country (any one which will have us).

I know you hated to give up your house, and I was sorry too, for I wanted to sneak in sometime and see how well you can cook. Congratulations on getting the promotion; I know you will be able to do any work which might be expected of you.

Man, I'll bet you are a powerful good chaperone! I would like to go on one of those parties; they sound like fun, especially the hayrides and watermelons.

Guess I had better quit now as I have to read all about the lens of the eye for tomorrow. Write again soon when you have some spare time.

Yours,

Ed

September 1, 1943

1.

Dear Wanda:

I believe you have the prettiest handwriting I have ever seen, and I surely do like to read it. That was a sweet long letter you wrote to me; I wish that I could think of that many interesting things to say. Last night I started a letter to you, but one of my good fraternity brothers came in, and the bull session lasted for into the night. I don't know how we can manage to waste so much time.

Last week the water finally cleared up in the Bay, and I caught two nice strings of fish. We had a fishing trip all planned Sunday morning, and we got up before daylight, and started out, but we could not find any bait in all of Galveston, so we came back home and went to bed.

Now it is the opening day of dove season in Dallas County and I am not there to help open it. I guess this is about the second time since I have been able to walk that I have missed opening day. I guess I will have to make up for lost time when I get out of school. The boy who started

EDMUND JONES
Archon

DAVID DAWSON
Vice-Archon

ALPHA KAPPA CHAPTER
PHI BETA PI

GALVESTON, TEXAS

BRUCE CAMERON
Secretary

ED ROWE
Treasurer

2.

the bull session last night has invited me to go home
with him this winter and do some duck hunting,
and I am planning big on that.

A little while ago I just came from the hospital
where I have been helping to take blood from
360 draftees. Boy, I thought they would never
quit coming through the door.

I have not heard from Pat and Bill for about
six months now. Bill was in the Air Corps Ground
School somewhere in Florida I believe, and Pat is
there with him.

For the past several days, I have been busy
writing out applications for internship. I want to go
to Parkland Hospital in Dallas, but I have applied
at Denver and Iowa City in case I do not
get in at Parkland. The Army allows us a year
for a civilian internship, during which time we
may go to any hospital in the country (any
one which will have us).

I know you hated to give up your house, and
I was sorry too, for I wanted to sneak in sometime

ALPHA KAPPA CHAPTER
PHI BETA PI

GALVESTON, TEXAS

3.

and see how good you can cook. Congratulation
on getting the promotion; I know you will be
able to do any work which might be expected
of you.

Man, I'll bet you are a powerful good chaperone!
I would like to go on one of those parties, they
sound like fun, especially the hayrides and
watermelons.

Guess I had better quit now, as I have to read
all about the lens of the eye for tomorrow. Write
again soon when you have some spare time.

Yours,
Ed.

October 20, 1943

Dear Wanda,

Please excuse the delay in writing to you. I have been real busy, and besides that, I am going to get myself all married up on October 28 in Austin. I hope that when you come to Dallas, we can all get together, for I know you would like Caroline. She is a med student in my class, and maybe, we will get to intern in Dallas together.

Tonight I have just been assigned a new patient at the children's hospital, and I have to go over and work him up pretty soon.

We are fixing up our fraternity house now, and last night, I painted so much I could scarcely stand up.

When do you think you will be going to Dallas? Be sure and let me know so I can get in touch with you next time I come home.

I hope everything is still going along well in Fairfield. I'll bet you will enjoy the football games this fall. Wish I could see some myself, but these Galveston teams always seem to play when I have the most work to do.

Guess I had better go up to the hospital now; be sure and write and let me know how everything is coming along.

Yours,
Ed

GALVESTON, TEXAS

Oct. 20, 1943

Dear Wanda:

Please excuse the delay in writing to you. I have been real busy, and besides that I am going to get myself all married up on Oct 28 in Austin. I hope that when you come to Dallas, we can all get together, for I know you would like Caroline. She is a med student in my class, and maybe we will get to intern in Dallas together.

Tonight I have just been assigned a new patient at the children's hospital, and I have to go over and work him up pretty soon.

We are fixing our fraternity house up now, and last night I painted so much I could scarcely stand up.

When do you think you will be going to Dallas; be sure and let me know, so I can

126

get in touch with you next time I came home.

I hope everything is still going along good in Fairfield. I'll bet you will enjoy the football games this fall. Wish I could see some myself, but these Galveston teams always seem to play when I have the most work to do.

Guess I had better go up to the hospital now; be sure and write and let me know how everything is coming along.

Yours,
Ed

Dear Wanda,

Thank you very much for your nice letter of about two months ago. I think that was the nicest letter I have gotten from anyone. Caroline said to tell you that she certainly does want to meet you.

Now I am at Jeff Davis Hospital in Houston, delivering babies. I will try to write you a real letter soon. Please let us hear from you sometime.

Ed

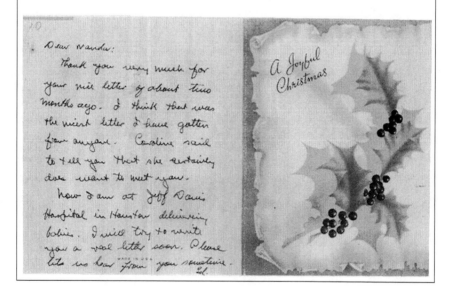

Edward B. Rowe, MD

Karen Paysse Rowe was born in 1951 on Galveston island, Texas. She now resides in Central Texas where she raises Dorper sheep and is involved in wildlife conservation.

She is the mother of four great adults who are the light of her life. Aside from family, her world is centered around travel, cooking, fun and laughter and a strong adoration for Jerry Lewis, who she believes encompasses all these things. In this book you will find love letters written by her father-in-law to one of his sweethearts in 1942. She kept these declarations of love for many years before passing them on to her after his death in 2002. Hope you enjoy this lost art of letterwriting.

The story takes place quite awhile ago. Long before a lot of us were born.

The writer of the letters is Ed.

He was studying medicine at the University of Texas Medical Branch in Galveston, and writing was second nature to him. He enjoyed the luxury of living on the Gulf Coast.

He spent many an afternoon swimming and fishing. Several days a week of dove and quail hunting on Bolivar Peninsula were not out of the ordinary for him. Sailing with his fraternity brothers was the usual Sunday afternoon outing.

Ed was fond of a lady friend that came from Wortham, Texas. She always welcomed his company. He spoke of visiting Wanda on his rail trips to call on his mom in Dallas. His mother always enjoyed his visits. He wrote Wanda letters, described his activities, and seemed to long for the day they could rendezvous. Their lives were busy and full of activities, which made it almost impossible. Wanda ended up saving Ed's letters. These are the letters he wrote to her.

Edwards Brothers Malloy
Oxnard, CA USA
April 29, 2015